Bright SY Flower

Tyrese Gould Jacinto

Illustrated by Arnild C. Aldepolla

The Way to Riches

Is What You Think

A Treatise

Dedication

I am dedicating this little treatise to my children; George, Annalyse, Adam, Sean, Marcus, Alex, Victor II, Brian, and Jordyn; my husband, Victor; my grandchildren Anastaysia, Nataliya, Caius, Atlas, and Jenavieve; my parents, Mark Gould and late Phyllis Mosley Gould Carter and my Grandmothers, the late Marion Gould, and Rebecca Loatman Mosley Seeney.

Contents

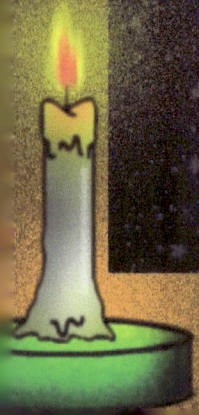

Acknowlegements

I want to say "thank you" to my husband and children for listening to my crazy thoughts, theories, dreams, visions, and putting up with my long discussions without calling the authorities to take me away. Sometimes I wonder how much I drove my Nana, Marion Gould, bonkers by calling her and visiting each time I came to a new realization or discovered a new (old) book or Sage. My Father, Mark, has always accepted my crazy way of "balanced" thinking and continues to support me, even though he sometimes doesn't agree. As all three of the strong women in my life have passed on, my mother, Phyllis, and my Grandmothers, Marion and Rebecca, continue to live within me. They all live through my children and grandchildren, and I see it every day.

Life is like a sandwich, and right now, I am in the middle!

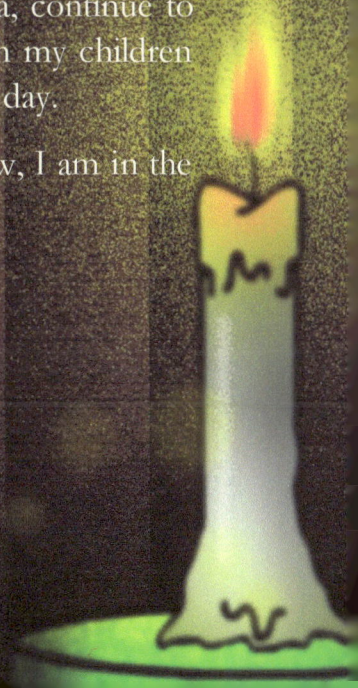

1

Beginning of Time

"Whenever I have encountered any problems, I have discovered that it is my own thinking 100% of the time. Whenever I have resolved any problems, I have discovered that it is my own thinking 100% of the time."

Tyrese Bright Flower Gould Jacinto 2015

The way to riches is what you think. This subject started over a conversation, and someone asked: "How do you have so much time to do the things, hobbies, and interests that you do"?

At that moment, I began to analyze that question and realized that I had not even noticed or considered what I do.

I concluded why I never pondered what I do: I never saw it in the way the question asked of me.

I believe that the only thing that we have is time. I see time as truly short and limited daily, but in a different manner. How I view time is that I do not like to "waste" time. I don't mean that I work 24-7 or around the clock; I mean that I am thinking while doing other things. I am a "thinking machine"!

It is not just about thinking random thoughts; however, it is about practicing controlled thinking. I learned at an exceedingly early age and realized that when I think, I create. When I create, I increase; when I grow, it makes me happy.

I am not talking about just riches. I never think about where my next meal is coming from or how much money I will make; I focus on the result of what I want to create.

Concentrated thought produces all the time. I will say that I am probably thinking every moment of my waking day, and even while I sleep.

My dreams are the result of controlled thinking. My thoughts turn into ideas that come to me in the middle of the night, and I quickly wake and write them down.

So, I know that my mind is thinking 100% of the time if I am breathing. I know that thinking things create things, and I know that I can think 100% of the time. It is a creative circle that produces an effect, creating something. If we look at it like this, all we have is time, and it becomes a beautiful concept.

So, while I do things like spending time watching movies, eating, on the farm, or in my shed, etc., I am also "spending" time thinking.

We would not want to spend our last dollars buying a rock if we are hungry; we want to spend them on food. And it is the same concept with time. All we have is time, and time is the only thing we do have.

So, when we say to spend your time wisely, it means that we all need to use our time to the fullest extent to shape our future. And using our time to the fullest to develop our future means thinking, or controlled thinking, all the time.

Let me go into further detail about spending. Why else would we say spend? We do not want to waste our time; we want to spend our time, but spend it wisely.

Even though we may have a lot of money to spend, we will still want to be frugal with our money and keep as much money as possible, just like time.

We do not want to spend or waste our money frivolously on things that we do not need or on overpriced items we do not like. And though we may get to the point where we have a lot of money to spend, we still want to spend wisely.

Spending our time wisely means being frugal with what we have earned and working to increase it. That is one of the other secrets of the way to riches. Being prudent with as much of our time and money as possible by using it wisely.

Everything in life begins with a thought. We think about it, take baby steps towards it without realizing, and then it just happens. Our whole world started as a thought.

When we rein in our thinking, we stop it from becoming random and control it. Then we begin to control our destiny.

We find ourselves taking steps towards that end goal without realizing that this is what we are doing.

And when we start thinking and controlling our thoughts, we find that we notice opportunities and doors opening because they are already part of our thought process, making us aware of what we are subconsciously looking for.

A Prayer for You

May the thoughts in your mind be good and kind.

May the dreams that please you, in time, come true.

May the happiness you earn help you to learn.

May the life that you live teach you to give.

Tyrese Bright Flower Gould 1978

2

The Test of Time

Many books, teachers, and great wise sages have analyzed why controlled thinking has been effective for thousands of years. I put it all to the test. I have read about synchronicity, about attraction laws, and I put it all to the test. I studied it, meditated on it, analyzed it, and concluded that it is not as difficult or as complicated as some would make it seem.

It is merely our thinking. My experience with the magnetic laws has been the result of my thinking 100% of the time and controlling it so that even when I dream, my thoughts or ideas begin to improve my life.

I spend time at work; I spend time at home. I spend time just like it is; I "spend" time wisely.

Controlling my thoughts means that I am aware that I am thinking, so as not to waste my time.

When watching a movie, I utilize my talents as a creator, blogger, or writer. I have my equipment with me, and while watching movies or doing other things, I create. By working simultaneously, I am not wasting any time and spending my time wisely.

Controlled thinking is just a note to everyone who asked where I get my time; you would be surprised what you can do during the day by thinking controllably.

Like anything else you learn, you will need to practice or exercise to control your thinking. If your mind wanders, bring it in, rein it in.

Thinking makes us aware of the opportunities and paths that lead to the baby steps we should subconsciously take. So, I have learned that controlling my thinking is what makes things happen.

I find this true with people as well. We learned that we attract what we are feeling inside, and I researched frequencies, which I believe in and will discuss further in this book.

Sometimes there is a force that we may not have control over. Still, in my experience with people, we may be in the company of their gloom or mostly miserable outlooks, and sometimes it is not because we have attracted them. Still, they are in our lives due to familial circumstances and are beyond our control.

We cannot control other people. However, we can control our thinking. In the beginning, I believed that these people were in my life because of my negative thinking. But I am rarely thinking negatively, and the same goes for miserable people. I was under the impression that I must be attracting them because I am miserable, but that is not the case. People are human and have emotions and feelings, and circumstances that affect their moods. When we understand that someone has mood-altering circumstances, we recognize that their feelings are just how they feel; we find compassion and realize that it most likely has little to do with us. We can stay positive.

I have discovered that I control what I feel and how I think. When gloomy or miserable people are around me, they cannot be sad or melancholic toward me because of my mindset. They diminished in their thoughts.

And my thinking and my presence, which is in love and acceptance, remains with me.

A cynical person finds it difficult to be negative in my presence; if they were and want to remain negative, they quickly leave my company. They are unable to withstand my positive and happy presence. I will do everything in my power to divert their negativity through my controlled thinking, ensuring positivity, and they have no choice but to find happiness within my presence or leave.

We attract happiness from others when we are happy. I always say that "everything is as it should be, and nothing is as it seems." My thinking is so powerful, and my attitude is so positive that, most of the time, others' emotions do not affect me. Positivity has taken many years of practice, but it is worth learning.

There was a person in my life whom I spoke to regularly. This person was usually terribly negative; however, when we had a conversation, they were always happy. When this person called someone else, it was in a very unhappy spirit.

When I spoke to the other person, we compared notes on the conversations; the person we talked to was so negative and unhappy with the other person, and happy while speaking to me.

This experience was not a strange occurrence; this is what attracted. We literally will attract what we are inside, whether that person is happy or negative. If we maintain a mindset of happiness and positivity, we will not allow others' negativity to affect us most of the time.

We cannot control the thinking of others, and others cannot control our thinking. However, our positive thinking will attract positivity in others.

We are thinking 100% of the time, and if we do not rein in our thinking to focus on the results we expect and continuously play in our head how we want something to be, then we have no idea of what we need.

All the awareness happens, and the mind opens to the right opportunities or paths for our baby steps. We take advantage of these opportunities when we control our thinking.

Steps of Life

As the whirlwind passes to give me breath,

I come into the world.

As I wade through the water near the shore,

I feel that I am me.

As I meet several seasons of the cold and heat,

I grow older and deeper in thought.

As I grow wiser and feel I am the bird of life,

I feed my family with knowledge.

As I sit by the big river and remember yesterday,

I think only good thoughts.

As I shut my eyes,

all is red.

The wind stops,

I will see you again!

Tyrese Bright Flower Gould 1979

3
Our Kingdom is Love

There are times when our thinking becomes out of control. We have found a great way to rein it back in, and this can be immensely powerful.

To get us into that correct line of thinking, we need to be in that place of love. This attracts all goodness that happens around us and in our lives. This form of love is hard to explain. However, it is how we choose to feel on the inside.

One verse I use to get back into that feeling when my thinking gets out of control, and I think about what I desire or do not have. This way of thinking is incorrect; it will give us a sense of lack, longing, loss, and unrest.

Sometimes our out-of-control thinking of desire will lead to depression. What I do to rein myself back in is I repeat this verse: "seek ye first the Kingdom of God and his righteousness, and these things shall be added unto me."

This verse is compelling, especially if you meditate on it day and night. When you seek first the Kingdom of God and his righteousness, you may conclude, as I have, that God is within us and "God" meaning the only power of love; when we seek "that" first and righteousness, which merely means 'doing the right thing in all things,' then those two things are added unto us!

Another powerful verse: The Kingdom of Heaven is at hand, can be interpreted as the love, peace, tranquility, and all good things through God within us, and are already with us.

If you add this verse to the verse as mentioned above, we can be in the actual state of love and realize that what we think, we have already added this unto us, which is what we are and will be.

When we think of those things and seek first the Kingdom of God and his righteousness, and know that the Kingdom of Heaven is at hand, then we realize we are in a state of love, satisfaction, and contentment, and through this power, all the things that we need, we will attract.

It is a beautiful cycle when we seek first the Kingdom of God and his righteousness and allow those things to be added unto us. It's not the things we are seeking; it is the Kingdom of God and his righteousness. So, we seek first the Kingdom of God and his righteousness, and these things are added unto us.

The Kingdom of God and the Kingdom of heaven, which is at hand, is the actual state of all acceptance and love. And when we experience the pure state of love, we have an unconditional way of thinking about everything. This pure thinking means that "everything is as it should be, and nothing is as it seems" will become our thinking.

Believing that "everything is as it should be, and nothing is as it seems" creates an inner spiritual magnet that subconsciously attracts whatever we need.

Whenever I have random thoughts and in a feeling of lack, I stop, and I think about how those things will be added unto me by seeking first the Kingdom and not by worrying about when, how, or why, which will delay the result.

This state of being and thinking fosters a genuine love for whatever surrounds you, attracting more of the same, which is true contentment. I already know in my heart that whatever I need in this pure state of thankfulness and love already shows up unconditionally and unconsciously.

Am I Really Me?

Am I what I appear to others?

I only please God to please others.

Am I what I really want to be?

I see myself as different,

for God made us original in our thoughts.

Do I respect and live a life of my own choice?

I respect how I live, for no one will respect me unless I have a life of my own.

But…

What does a deaf man see in my actions?

What does a blind man hear in the words I speak?

Does an introverted man think of me

With good thoughts?

Asking these questions, I wonder….

Am I really me?

Tyrese Bright Flower Gould 1980

4
Master of Your Feelings

This chapter is mainly about our feelings. We go through life with emotions and feelings every day. But it is a simple act to maintain your feelings, but only after you recognize that your feelings are "your feelings."

I will explain the feeling of love. Love is how we control our emotions when external forces make us feel for, or because of, the actions of others.

You will have an aha moment. Your feelings are your feelings, no matter what, period! If someone does something to upset you, you analyze what bothers you. If someone is displeased with what you are doing, you must break it down and analyze their uneasiness with what you are doing and separate yourself from their judgment.

Feeling love for someone else and feeling love, in general, is just what it is. You are the one feeling it. You cannot feel the love that someone else has for you, and you can only feel the love you generate that you have, and that is all that matters.

It does not matter if someone has love; you are the only one who truly matters, and you experience what love is.

If you feel love and what love is, then that is the main attractor. The feeling of love is the highest form and the highest attractor of peace that we will have.

Once you are again satisfied with yourself and your actions, it is easier to stay in that entire state of love and acceptance.

That feeling of love is because you feel love. When you are upset at someone because you think they have offended you and separate yourself from their actions, you become confident in what you are doing. You can remain in a steady state of love and acceptance, which overrides any feelings caused by external forces.

If you get hurt by someone else, and if that person who hurt you is unhappy with your actions, that person has feelings of unhappiness.

That unhappiness does not have to be your unhappiness; you can stay in the state of love, and that person will be affected by their despair.

If someone is jealous, then that person feels the feeling of jealousy, which does not have to affect you if you are staying in the state of love.

If that person feels hate or contempt for you, you do not feel that hate or disgust. That person is experiencing those feelings of hatred or contempt.

The examples go on and on. You are the master of your feelings, no matter the external circumstances, barring physical hurt, but mental pain does not have to be. You don't have to get hurt because of another person's actions; you can still feel love.

You are the only one who can feel love. The other person cannot feel your love. The other people in your life must feel their own love or whatever emotions they feel.

If someone feels disgusted by something that you do, you do not have to feel the effects of their disgust. It does not affect you in any way, shape, or form.

Your actions are your actions, and their actions are their actions. Your feelings are your feelings, and their feelings are their feelings. It is as simple as that.

If you stay in a steady state of love, others' actions and feelings mentally do not affect you, and if they do, you can practice turning them around very quickly.

When we learn to accept others and their feelings as they are, we can separate ourselves from them as individuals, and therefore, we can stay in the steady state of true love.

When we realize that we all face consequences or rewards for our actions, we limit or eliminate others' judgments and accept others as they are.

There is no clear right or wrong. There are laws to maintain, but there is no right or wrong within the laws of feelings. What we are pleased with and what codes we live by possibly will not matter to how others live.

We must maintain our processes and codes, and morality, and morals, and sense of citizenship. When we hold ourselves and look within, we do not notice others' things, even if they are directed to hurt us.

Hurt happens in relationships every day. When people have formed relationships, no matter what type of bond it is, they have a bond based on their feelings.

We cannot feel the feelings of others. We can only feel our emotions, so when someone says, "I don't love you anymore," and they want to end whatever that relationship is, their love effect is not affecting your state of love, but it is affecting another person, even though you may be hurt.

Yes, life changes could occur, such as families breaking up, death, or changing jobs; but you can still feel that state of love, primarily if the love is directed towards everything.

When we begin to impose our beliefs on others, it simply means that we are not looking within to our feelings and letting the choices of others dictate what we feel.

When we let ourselves be affected by others and not be in a state of love, we will not impose our beliefs. Others may not believe the same way. When we see the result that we feel that we should have, by attempting to convince our thoughts, we open ourselves up to millions of emotions, and each one of those emotions is one step away from the natural feeling of love.

Once we accept others and the situation as "it is what it is," and we look within, we become satisfied with our own beliefs, and we can stay in that actual state of feeling the love.

When we are in the actual state of love, we realize that we want to be genuinely happy. We want that same happiness for everyone else that we encounter. We want them to be satisfied. We want them to ride with the dog hanging out of the window, we want them to live in the city or the country, and we want them to travel around the world, or whatever, if what they are doing, whatever it is, makes them happy.

When their feelings are happy, that is what love is, a total acceptance of others, and what makes them happy because we have found happiness when we are in an entire state of love.

Holy Nature; Ease in My Mind

World of unity, ease in my mind, a pretend mind of great ignorance, but holy wisdom is truth. It seems a world I barely know projects on a world I wanted, yet I have.

Strapped within the pressure, I am drowning in sheets of metal and buried beneath the unbalanced wilderness in physicality. Must I dig? How must I be aware? Am I living in a world of forgiveness and loving a world of truth, and unity equals the ease in my mind?

Is it unity when I stand as tall as the tallest tree and sleep curled as though I am a born-again child? Is it not a world of unity?

As I am dressed in holy nature, love that is deeply hidden behind all true feelings and rules of the right actions.

It is like a vast blanket of cement over large masses of earth, yet it is like a flock of gulls flying high above.

I wear love as though I am wearing my finest cloth, and love is my only nature.

Each day, it is fed to me, one bite at a time. It nourishes my hunger like a new bird that is being fed by its true loving mother.

The fixation of smiles on my face reveals moments, experiences, actions, as though I am saying, "I have no hate in my heart, but holy nature; love."

Am I but a rope of love, each weak thread woven to make one strong thread? I am dressed in holy nature.

Is my soul the cause of real-world unity? It is like being on a large and high mountain, with a foundation of love.

It is though I have paddled between two meaningful worlds. Worlds I understand, which causes my holy nature to be dressed. Must I dig? Must I choose?

Must I choose between a world that I wanted and a world I barely know?

The meat of which condenses my deepest real values is screaming to be mended without falsehoods, but of truth! It's screaming I am healed with love.

Holy nature, which is caused by my world of unity, is the ease in my mind.
Tyrese Bright Flower Gould 1982

5
Balance

We take the word balance very lightly, but do we know what it means? Balance is a heavily loaded concept that I am going to try to explain.

We can explain balance like this: when we say that we need to have balance in life, it is for us to succeed in life; we must control our emotions and actions, and live the best way possible that leads us to happiness.

Balance is a mixture of many different concepts, including color, light, sound frequency, developing our chakra skills, and building our character through controlled thinking and doing.

Let us consider color. Color is not what we think it is. The color we see is the absence of the color that is revealed to us.

The surface of the object reflects the wavelengths we see as color and absorbs all the rest. An object appears white when it reflects all wavelengths and black when it absorbs them all.

What is in the middle? Green! We find that the color green is in the middle, and because green is in the middle, it is the balance of the color spectrum. So, if green is the balance of the colors, we can associate green with various reasons for balance.

We cannot see the green unless we have all the colors from the spectrum, from the bottom of reds to the top of violets. When we balance all the colors from red to violet, the middle is green.

Consider how color works. The absence of color is when we see green. We recognize all the colors of the spectrum except green.

So green is a profound concept of balance. It is no mistake that the ancient peoples would use the term that they "see green" in people, meaning that they envy or see green in their eyes, which indicates that they are probably out of balance with envious emotions.

As referred to in jealousy, green is the lack of or the opposite of love or total acceptance, and reflects the absence of the green wavelength that consists of the green spectrum, which is a balance, which is why we can see it.

A word of caution. We must be mindful that we do not recognize our own imbalance of green that we see in others. Sometimes, if we see others in a negative aspect, we may be familiar with the lack that is deep inside us.

Sometimes, if we see green in others, it may be that we can only recognize in others how it is in ourselves. Therefore, we could be looking at our own out-of-balance color as well as theirs. Because we can only see the color that is missing in us, we notice the green or the imbalance we have as well.

The same holds if we do not know the color that exists: the balance of both ends of the spectrum or all the colors described as having whole light.

When we consider all the colors mixed, we emit that which is light. This mix of colors is what we refer to as the light that shines within us.

When we think of color as a wavelength, the lowest color,

red, bounces on a very slow frequency, and the very top of the color spectrum, which is violet, reflects on a very rapid frequency. Either of these ends of the spectrum is out of balance.

If we find the center of the wave links, we see the balance and balance of the green spectrum wavelengths.

Therefore, we want to become balanced with our wavelength and frequencies and remain balanced; we must radiate and be full of light in the middle.

Everything has the opposite. Whenever we get pulled to the extreme opposite, we subconsciously gravitate to the balance in the middle. If you are sad, you will need to find a way to be the happy opposite. However, attempting to maintain a balance with too much happiness will cause you to tip the balance back towards sadness. It is excellent to practice being balanced. There are many examples of emotional balance that you can meditate on, and I do not need to explain each.

Karmic balance story:

I received a call from a friend. This person was venting, and all I remember saying was, "I can only worry about my karma and balance!"

That night, I had a very vivid dream. I have many dreams, and most of them I can remember. At times, I will get up and write down the details immediately.

In this dream, I was instructed to create the yin-yang drawing, put a line directly through from top to bottom, and from side to side, and analyze the picture. I quickly noticed that the spot in the center did not pass through the black or white, and with the lines drawn, it came to me that if we are out of balance ever so slightly, we will need to swing back to fulfill the need for balance. However, if we stay directly in the center of the chart and do not stray from the center, there is no need to swing to become balanced.

For me, this is a revelation and a new task that I must now practice. I tend to get emotional or react at times in different situations.

Now that I am aware of this revelation, I can suddenly stop the emotional sway that would lead me away from the center balance.

Walk with Me

To the North

Reach your arms high to the sun,

Give praise and thanks,

For he provides till day is done.

Feel his warmth and beauty shine,

Now I know his love is mine.

Walk with me, and you shall see!

To the East

Neal, bow down to Mother Earth,

For she provides food and shelter,

And all your love.

Protect the ways in which she lives,

Learn the ways in which she gives.

Fear her wisdom, strength, and power,

Neal, bow down for now is the hour.

Walk with me, and you shall see!

To the South

Turn your face up to the rain,

It's gentle and soft; you feel no pain.

Each little drop, one by one,

Quenches the thirst of Mother Earth,

Beneath the great sun.

Gentle and soft as it may seem,

Without its touch, lakes, rivers, and oceans,

could not be.

Walk with me, and you shall see!

To the West

Look ahead it's running free,

Wildlife beautiful and stunning to see.

Amazing the unsure,

But the sure way of surviving;

Through Mother Earth,

The keeper of all,

The balance all living styles.

Walk with me, and you shall see;

Love, peace, and harmony.

I thank him for a job well done.

I praise Him, the Great Spirit,

the perfect one.

Tyrese Bright Flower Gould 1989

6
Wholly Trinity

When we think of the Holy Trinity, our mind wanders toward the teachings of the Bible. Instead, we will define and focus on another concept, which is "wholly trinity", in this chapter, related to the body, soul, and spirit.

Within our wholly trinity, when we speak of balance, we must be mindful of our body, soul, and spirit, and the health thereof, to be able to attract the goodness that we need.

The healthy body is not what we refer to as the outward appearance; what we see on the outward appearance can only be or may only be a facade of what is really inside our body.
We can be the most beautiful tree with the most beautiful

bark with the most beautiful leaves, and if we do not bear fruit, what good are we? If we bear fruit, that is the most beautiful fruit, yet when we open that fruit, we find that the fruit inside is rotten; what good are we?

We can use this analogy for the body. Although the external appearance results from what we have inside, we are not defined solely by our outward appearance. We must take care of our bodies by eating wholesome foods, avoiding anything considered poisonous, processed foods with high metal content as preservatives, and destructive drinks.

When we take care of our bodies, then our bodies will necessarily take care of us. We desire to wake up every single day pain-free, feeling alive, alert, and ready for whatever the day has in store for us.

There is one thing that I always like to say, and that is, "it's only about today."

When we talk about the soul, we speak of how we feed our soul; our personality, ego, likes, and dislikes. What I mean by that is that we must surround ourselves with wisdom and knowledge. Wisdom from all walks of life spiritually to become that righteous soul.

When we hear words, we quickly paint a mental picture as we hear the words spoken. It is essential only to listen to words that are edifying to our souls and spirits. Word simply means sound frequency.

When we refer to our soul, we say I or I am. The word I, simply means self-consciousness or ego. The word "am" merely means "present" or "to be."

It is no accident that the words "I am" are also close in sound frequency to the words Amen, which is a chant of thankfulness, and ohm, which is a chant for balance and peace.

It also mentioned that "I am" can be referred to as God or the God within us in several books.

Here are a few verses that pertain to words and sound frequency: (King James Version):

For the word of God is quick and powerful, and sharper than any two-edged sword, piercing even to the dividing asunder of soul and spirit, and of the joints and marrow, and is a discerner of the thoughts and intents of the heart.

Hebrews 4:12

All scripture is given by inspiration of God, and is profitable for doctrine, for reproof, for correction, for instruction in righteousness: That the man of God may be perfect, thoroughly furnished unto all good works.

2 Timothy 3:16-17

Thy word is a lamp unto my feet, and a light unto my path.

Psalm 119:105

But be ye doers of the word, and not hearers only, deceiving your own selves.

James 1:22

Wherewithal shall a young man cleanse his way? By taking heed thereto according to thy word.

Psalm 119:9

The grass withereth, the flower fadeth: but the word of our God shall stand for ever.

Isaiah 40:8

But he said, Yea rather, blessed are they that hear the

word of God, and keep it.

Luke 11:28

Therefore whosoever heareth these sayings of mine, and doeth them, I will liken him unto a wise man, which built his house upon a rock.

Matthew 7:24

As for God, his way is perfect: the word of the Lord is tried: he is a buckler to all those that trust in him.

Psalm 18:30

Do all things without murmurings and disputing's: That ye may be blameless and harmless, the sons of God, without rebuke, in the midst of a crooked and perverse nation, among whom ye shine as lights in the world; Holding forth the word of life.

Philippians 2:14-16a

Heaven and earth shall pass away, but my words shall not pass away.

Matthew 24:35

The entrance of thy words giveth light; it giveth

understanding unto the simple.

Psalm 119:130

But he answered and said, it is written, Man shall not live by bread alone, but by every word that proceedeth out of the mouth of God.

Matthew 4:4

In the beginning was the Word, and the Word was with God, and the Word was God.

John 1:1

For the word of the Lord is right; and all his works are done in truth.

Psalm 33:4

He that believeth on me, as the scripture hath said, out of his belly shall flow rivers of living water.

John 7:38

In God I will praise his word, in God I have put my trust;

I will not fear what flesh can do unto me.

Psalm 56:4

As newborn babes, desire the sincere milk of the word, that ye may grow thereby.

1 Peter 2:2

For the Lord giveth wisdom: out of his mouth cometh knowledge and understanding.

Proverbs 2:6

Then said Jesus to those Jews which believed on him, if ye continue in my word, then are ye my disciples indeed; and ye shall know the truth, and the truth shall make you free.

John 8:31-32

Wherefore lay apart all filthiness and superfluity of naughtiness, and receive with meekness the engrafted word, which is able to save your souls.

James 1:21

And he humbled thee, and suffered thee to hunger, and fed thee with manna, which thou knewest not, neither did thy fathers know; that he might make thee know that man doth not live by bread only, but by every word that proceedeth out of the mouth of the Lord doth man live.

Deuteronomy 8:3

Thou hast also given me the shield of thy salvation: and thy right hand hath holden me up, and thy gentleness hath made me great. Thou hast enlarged my steps under me, that my feet did not slip.

Psalm 18:35-36

And the Word was made flesh, and dwelt among us, (and we beheld his glory, the glory as of the only begotten of the Father,) full of grace and truth.

John 1:14

Who being the brightness of his glory, and the express image of his person, and upholding all things by the word of his power, when he had by himself purged our sins, sat down on the right hand of the Majesty on high.

Hebrews 1:3

Thou art my hiding place and my shield:

I hope in thy word.

Psalm 119:114

If ye abide in me, and my words abide in you, ye shall ask what ye will, and it shall be done unto you.

John 15:7

Thy word is true from the beginning: and every one of thy righteous judgments endureth for ever.

Psalm 119:160

So shall my word be that goeth forth out of my mouth: it shall not return unto me void, but it shall accomplish that which I please, and it shall prosper in the thing whereto I sent it.

Isaiah 55:11

I wait for the Lord, my soul doth wait, and in his word do I hope.

Psalm 130:5

Every word of God is pure: he is a shield unto them that put their trust in him.

Proverbs 30:5

Thy word have I hid in mine heart, that I might not sin against thee.

Psalm 119:11

Let the word of Christ dwell in you richly in all wisdom; teaching and admonishing one another in psalms and hymns and spiritual songs, singing with grace in your hearts to the Lord.

Colossians 3:16

Being born again, not of corruptible seed, but of incorruptible, by the word of God, which liveth and abideth for ever.

1 Peter 1:23

For the scripture saith, whosoever believeth on him shall not be ashamed.

Romans 10:11

And he was there with the Lord forty days and forty nights; he did neither eat bread, nor drink water. And he wrote upon the tables the words of the covenant, the Ten Commandments.

Exodus 34:28

Faithful is he that calleth you, who also will do it.

1 Thessalonians 5:24

As for God, his way is perfect; the word of the Lord is tried: he is a buckler to all them that trust in him.

2 Samuel 22:31

Neither have I gone back from the commandment of his lips;

I have esteemed the words of his mouth more than my necessary food.

Job 23:12

It is a faithful saying: For if we be dead with him, we shall also live with him.

2 Timothy 2:11

The law of the Lord is perfect, converting the soul: the testimony of the Lord is sure, making wise the simple.

Psalm 19:7

Quotes by Tyrese Gould Jacinto

"We begin to lose our way when the objective of the object becomes a pleasure instead of usefulness. The same holds when we begin to use our religion as God instead of God." 2019

"Never think of the future and forget the past, and your future will someday be past." 1995

"I am faithful in my little things, and the Great Spirit blesses me with much." 1996

"You can only recognize in me what spirits you know in yourself." 1997

"You take you with you." 2004

"I won't let you go; I set you free!" 2009

7

My Nana and I

My Nana and I enjoyed many in-depth discussions about wisdom. Each time I discovered a new work of history and faith, I would buy one book for each of us.

As we read, I had many questions. I remember asking my Nana and then telling her my opinion. She would always say, "I suppose that's possible."

The last book was the Nag Hammadi Library, which consists of 2,000-year-old papyrus scriptures found in an alabaster jar in Egypt in 1945. Now that I look back, I see that I have discovered something extraordinary about my Nana. I have meditated on this for a few months, and it was the first thing I pondered when I was 12.

When things come full circle, we know it is for a reason.

Nana spoke with the tongues of men and of angels. Nana had the gift of prophecy, understood all mysteries and knowledge, and had faith so that she could remove mountains.

Nana fed the poor.

Nana suffered long, and she was kind; Nana was not jealous; Nana was humble.

Nana carried herself gracefully, and she always thought of others; she was not easily provoked, and she thought well of all.

Nana rejoiced in the truth.

Nana bore all things, she believed all things, she hoped all things, and she endured all things.

In short, my Nana had Charity!

1 Corinthians 13 (King James Version) is my latest meditation, and it reads:

1. *Though I speak with the tongues of men and of angels, and have not charity, I am become as sounding brass, or a tinkling cymbal.*

2. *And though I have the gift of prophecy, and understand all mysteries, and all knowledge; and though I have all faith, so that I could remove mountains, and have not charity, I am nothing.*

3. *And though I bestow all my goods to feed the poor, and though I give my body to be burned, and have not charity, it profiteth me nothing.*

4. *Charity suffereth long, and is kind; charity envieth not; charity vaunteth not itself, is not puffed up,*

5. *Doth not behave itself unseemly, seeketh not her own, is not easily provoked, thinketh no evil;*

6. *Rejoiceth not in iniquity, but rejoiceth in the truth;*

7. *Beareth all things, believeth all things, hopeth all things, endureth all things.*

8. *Charity never faileth: but whether there be prophecies, they shall fail; whether there be tongues, they shall cease; whether there be knowledge, it shall vanish away.*

9. *For we know in part, and we prophesy in part.*

10. *But when that which is perfect is come, then that which is in part shall be done away.*

When I was a child, I spake as a child, I understood as a child, I thought as a child: but when I became a man,

11. *I put away childish things.*

12. *For now we see through a glass, darkly; but then face to face: now I know in part; but then shall I know even as also I am known.*

13. *And now abideth faith, hope, charity, these three; but the greatest of these is charity.*

With this, all I can say is that my Nana, Marion Doris Purnell Gould, was an enlightened soul and beautiful spirit.

The following is a poem that I wrote to represent our relationship and includes both of our Native American spiritual given names:

Medicine Flower - A Lenape legend

In blessed sun

and during rain,

springs the blossom

that heals our pain.

with its "Strong Medicine"

and a "Bright Flower",

brings the gift

through God's power.

this we know as the

"Medicine Flower".

Tyrese Bright Flower Gould – Lenape 1998

8

Displeasing Others

Life has a way of throwing little lessons, and one new set of events taught me a valuable lesson.

I have always known that it is a disaster to try to please others who might be displeased with what you do, to please someone else. The other person is annoyed, and this cycle goes on.

But do we practice what we preach? I found that I say this often, but I do just the opposite. It usually becomes a disaster in my thinking because I feel that I have fallen short of someone. However, if I do 100% for someone and it does not turn out, I do not fall short, while my actions are 100% to please God.

Sometimes our 100% is not what someone needs. And if the one asking does not need what we have to offer, that does not mean that we fail. It just simply means that we cannot serve that which is sought. If we are doing 100%, then we did not fail, but we have succeeded.

It is not a failure if you are doing 100% because it is your duty.

There are times when I feel that I did not fulfill someone's wishes. If someone is disappointed with the results of what I can do for them, I step back, and I analyze why I feel bad.

I always come up with the same conclusion each time after meditating on why I have hurt feelings. My end draws my attention to the fact that it has nothing to do with my emotions. But it has everything to do with my ability to perform to someone with their expectations.

It is not a failure if we do 100% best. And those expectations do not meet someone else's expectations. It has no loss if someone is disappointed in what we do; if we do our best, the fault is only in our heads.

Our sense of feeling is our thinking. It is not a failure. If we are not doing whatever responsibility is to 100%, it is not a failure. If the outcome does not meet the expectations, it is not a failure if we perform to the best of our ability. If the actions that we are doing or pleasing someone, we can never please anyone.

We cannot make anyone happy; every person oversees their happiness. Everyone is in charge of their destination. Every person manages their joy.

I monitor my joy. My response makes me happy. I am pleased to know that I did all that I could do to fulfill my duties and responsibilities at the end of the day.

I have no remorse, am not upset, and do not have animosity for anyone. I know that I am happy at the end of the day because I did all I could. Therefore, this is the lesson that sometimes, things do not seem to go right. And that, although someone may be disappointed in what we do, we must sit back. And we must analyze.

We cannot make others happy. We can only be happier ourselves. And being glad ourselves means that we do 100% that day. I am going to do 100% to please God.

Because if I try to make you happy, then he is displeased. If I try to make the displeased one happy, then you are upset.

But if I try to do everything in my power to make God happy, then all I must be concerned with is God.

9
Throw in the Towel

A hard-learned lesson. This day was a beautiful day. We woke up early, had many things to do on our list, and we're accomplishing all.

It was hot outside; however, everything went well. We were in and out throughout the day as if we were tag-teaming the house.

But it was a good time, we felt accomplished and successful, and we are enjoying ourselves. I received great news about an appointment the next day, Sunday, which brought great joy and a small amount of excitement and fear because it was something new that would be my task.

I clearly remember being in and out of my bathroom throughout the day between the chores. I took my contacts out early and continued my day.

In the evening, when I used the bathroom, I noticed that my towel was missing. I did not see it missing earlier in the day when I was in and out because it is positioned next to the door, right next to the light switch, next to my sink, and it would be hard to miss if it were missing earlier.

So, I looked around the bedroom. I looked around the house, and I could not find my towel.

Two of the three sons were home; however, we did not see one son throughout the day.

So, I asked my sons, "What did you do with my towel?" They replied, "What towel?" I told him that my bath towel was hanging in my bathroom and demanded what he did with my towel.

So, I called the other son who was not at home and asked him the same question What did you do with my towel? And he said I did not do anything with your towel.

At that very moment, panic set in. This was just not any towel; this was a bath sheet towel, and not only any bath sheet towel; this was a gift from my mother, the Christmas before she passed away.

She gave my husband and me a set of towels, very luxurious, large bath sheet towels.

When I used this towel each morning, I would just think about how my mother liked nice things and how these towels were so lovely.

Much to my surprise, I was emotional; I was attached to this towel. My world fell apart. I had an important meeting the next day; the goats were due for their shots that day, and we had an appointment across town that morning as well.

It is after 11 o'clock p.m., and I am going crazy about my towel. My husband and my sons were frantically looking for this towel with me, and we could not find it anywhere.

It is now 12:30 a.m. I sit in a living room chair like a little child who lost her blanket because I could not find my towel.

Since it was so late and my teachings of never going to bed angry came into play, I quickly changed my emotions to sadness, extreme sadness, and went to bed.

I fell asleep, but I remembered waking up from time to time with a heavy heart and many thoughts of what could have happened to my towel.

I thought maybe it met its demise at the hands of one of my children, and it was ruined and thrown away, and they were trying to save my feelings.

I thought about a robber coming into my home and stealing my towel. I thought about my oldest son using it to go to the pool and many other things.

While I did not get much sleep, and morning came, I said my usual prayers, and I added, "Lord, why do I feel this way about my towel"? And I asked what this lesson you want me to learn about this loss that I feel about my towel is about?

I know that this is a strange story to place at the end of this book; however, it is in line with thinking concepts.

I thought about the towel as if it were more than the usefulness of being a towel. Thinking of objects as more than they are will block our way to our objectives and blessings. All things are made to be useful, and when they are no longer useful, they are to be retired.

The object is not the person, nor does it take the place of any living thing of importance in our lives. When we hold onto an object for the wrong reasons, we block opportunities for replacements.

When I finally realized that I had an emotional attachment to a silly towel, it became just that, a towel. I realized that there were more opportunities to think about my mother than when using the towel.

Not only that, while shopping in a local store, I stumbled on a sale of the same towels in many different colors. Had I held the unhealthy attachment to this object, I most likely would not have noticed that there were replacements.

Letting go of objects that have surpassed their effectiveness opens the doors for more opportunities. Thinking of the loss blocked the way to the new blessings ahead.

Now I use the term "throw in the towel" as a metaphor for many aspects of life and work. I also use the phrase "give up", as to say, give it to the Creator. As soon as I do, the answers appear.